EYEWITNESS TO HISTORY

ELIZABETH CADY STANTON

in her own words

Gareth Stevens
PUBLISHING

By Nicole Shea

Please visit our website, www.garethstevens.com. For a free color catalog of all our high-quality books, call toll free 1-800-542-2595 or fax 1-877-542-2596.

Library of Congress Cataloging-in-Publication Data

Shea, Nicole.
Elizabeth Cady Stanton in her own words / by Nicole Shea.
p. cm. — (Eyewitness to history)
Includes index.
ISBN 978-1-4824-1288-8 (pbk.)
ISBN 978-1-4824-1201-7 (6-pack)
ISBN 978-1-4824-1478-3 (library binding)
1. Stanton, Elizabeth Cady, — 1815-1902 — Juvenile literature. 2. Suffragists — United States — Biography — Juvenile literature. 3. Women — Suffrage — United States — Juvenile literature. I. Shea, Nicole, 1976-. II. Title.
HQ1413.S67 S46 2015
324.6—d23

First Edition

Published in 2015 by
Gareth Stevens Publishing
111 East 14th Street, Suite 349
New York, NY 10003

Copyright © 2015 Gareth Stevens Publishing

Designer: Katelyn E. Reynolds
Editor: Therese Shea

Photo credits: Cover, p. 1 (Elizabeth) sconosciuto/Wikipedia.com; cover, p. 1 (background illustration) FPG/Getty Images; cover, p. 1 (logo quill icon) Seamartini Graphics Media/Shutterstock.com; cover, p. 1 (logo stamp) YasnaTen/Shutterstock.com; cover, p. 1 (color grunge frame) DmitryPrudnichenko/Shutterstock.com; cover, pp. 1–32 (paper background) Nella/Shutterstock.com; cover, pp. 1–32 (decorative elements) Ozerina Anna/Shutterstock.com; pp. 1–32 (wood texture) Reinhold Leitner/Shutterstock.com; pp. 1–32 (open book background) Elena Schweitzer/Shutterstock.com; pp. 1–32 (bookmark) Robert Adrian Hillman/Shutterstock.com; p. 5 Time Life Pictures/Mansell/Getty Images; p. 7 Binksternet/Wikipedia.com; pp. 8, 15 Hulton Archive/Getty Images; pp. 8–9 Given by British and Foreign Anti-Slavery Society, 1880/National Portrait Gallery, London/Wikipedia.com; pp. 11 (both), 21 courtesy of Library of Congress; p. 13 Engraved by G.E. Perine & Co., NY/Wikipedia.com; p. 17 U.S. National Archives and Records Administration/Wikipedia.com; pp. 18, 27 Library of Congress/Wikipedia.com; p. 19 Bilpen/Wikipedia.com; pp. 22–23 PhotoQuest/Getty Images; p. 25 Univeral History Archive/UIG/Getty Images; p. 27 (signature) Scewing/Wikipedia.com.

Printed in the United States of America

CPSIA compliance information: Batch #CS15GS: For further information contact Gareth Stevens, New York, New York at 1-800-542-2595.

CONTENTS

*Words in the glossary appear in **bold** type the first time they are used in the text.*

EARLY *Years*

Elizabeth Cady was born November 12, 1815, in Johnstown, New York, to Margaret Livingston and Daniel Cady. In an account of her life, Elizabeth remembered her mother as a *"tall, queenly"* woman of great courage. Her father was a gentle man who was a lawyer and later judge. However, Elizabeth learned very early that her father had wanted another son and not a daughter. In fact, she came to know that to many people at that time, *"girls were considered an inferior order of beings."*

In the early 1800s, women had few rights. Most couldn't own property, and they couldn't vote. Women couldn't go to college or pursue most careers. Instead, they were taught how to become good wives and mothers. All her life, Elizabeth, later known as Elizabeth Cady Stanton, fought this unfair treatment.

Elizabeth Cady Stanton was born into a wealthy family with social status. However, she still felt at a disadvantage being a girl.

"I WISH YOU WERE A BOY!"

At a young age, Elizabeth was unhappy that she was born a girl. When she was 11, her only brother died shortly after graduating from college. Her father was inconsolable. When Elizabeth tried to comfort him, *"At length he heaved a deep sigh and said: 'Oh, my daughter, I wish you were a boy!' Throwing my arms about his neck, I replied: 'I will try to be all my brother was.'"*

5

HENRY STANTON, ABOLITIONIST

Elizabeth was impressed by Henry Stanton's speaking skills and his ideas for ending slavery. They married in 1840. She refused to give up her last name completely, choosing to be called "Elizabeth Cady Stanton" rather than "Mrs. Henry Stanton." The common phrase "promise to obey" was left out of their wedding vows at her request. She later wrote, *"I obstinately refused to obey one with whom I supposed I was entering into an equal relation."*

Elizabeth excelled in school to make her father proud. In fact, she was the only girl in some of her classes at Johnstown Academy. After graduation, most of the boys went to Union College in Schenectady, New York. *"Those with whom I had studied and contended for prizes for five years came to bid me good-by, and I learned of the barrier that prevented me from following in their footsteps—'no girls admitted here.'"* No US college allowed women to study with men at that time.

In 1830, Elizabeth began to attend Troy Female **Seminary**. This institution had classes similar to those in men's colleges. She received one of the best educational experiences available. After she graduated, Elizabeth became involved in the antislavery and **temperance** movements. Through these activities, she met her future husband, Henry Stanton.

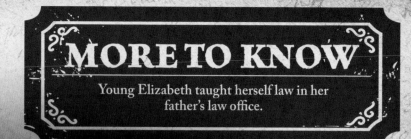

MORE TO KNOW

Young Elizabeth taught herself law in her father's law office.

Henry Stanton was a powerful speaker for the abolitionist, or antislavery, movement.

THE WORLD'S
Antislavery Convention

Soon after Elizabeth and Henry's wedding, they traveled to London, England, so Henry could attend the World's Antislavery **Convention**. Elizabeth discovered that women weren't allowed to participate in the meeting, even though some had been elected as delegates to attend. Elizabeth had to sit at the rear of the hall, while her husband was seated with the men.

MORE TO KNOW

Lucretia Mott was a well-known abolitionist and women's rights supporter when she arrived in London for the convention as one of six female delegates.

Elizabeth was deeply hurt *"that abolitionists, who felt so keenly the wrongs of the slave, should be so **oblivious** to the equal wrongs of their own mothers, wives, and sisters."* Her anger was shared by a new friend, Lucretia Mott, who was a delegate. The women promised *"to hold a convention as soon as we returned home, and form a society to **advocate** the rights of women,"* Elizabeth recalled.

ONBOARD BEHAVIOR

On their way to England, Elizabeth was criticized for her unwomanly behavior. She had played tag with her brother-in-law on deck. She allowed the captain to lift her chair up to the mast on a dare. She also called her husband "Henry" in front of other passengers and not "Mr. Stanton." Elizabeth tried to act the part of the wife of an important representative of the antislavery movement, but she was her usual, lively self.

The World's Antislavery Convention met between June 12 and June 23 in 1840.

9

The SENECA FALLS *Convention*

FREDERICK DOUGLASS

Among the men in the audience at the convention was Frederick Douglass, a former slave and abolitionist. He believed that slaves and women had a lot in common. Douglass supported the idea that women should be allowed to vote. He later wrote, *"The right of women to vote is as sacred in my judgment as that of men, and I am quite willing at any time to hold up both hands in favor of this right."*

The women's rights convention took place 8 years later, in 1848, in Seneca Falls, New York. This was the town in which Elizabeth Cady Stanton lived, then raising three young boys. She, Lucretia Mott, and three other women worked on a statement for the convention that they called the Declaration of Sentiments. It was a statement of complaints and demands patterned after the Declaration of Independence.

Some people said the declaration went too far when it asked for the right to vote. However, in a speech on July 19, Stanton stated that women already had the right to vote as US citizens: *"Strange as it may seem to many, we now demand our right to vote according to the declaration of the government under which we live... The right is ours. Have it, we must. Use it, we will."*

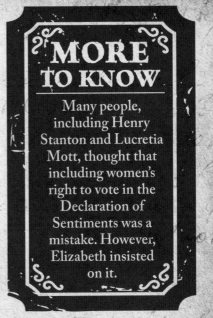

This card was issued for the celebration held at Seneca Falls in 1908 and is added to by Harriet Stanton Blatch.

Our Roll of Honor

Containing all the

Signatures to the "Declaration of Sentiments"
Set Forth by the First

Woman's Rights Convention,

held at
Seneca Falls, New York
July 19-20, 1848.

LADIES:

Lucretia Mott
Harriet Cady Eaton
Margaret Pryor
Elizabeth Cady Stanton
Eunice Newton Foote
Mary Ann M'Clintock
Margaret Schooley
Martha C. Wright
Jane C. Hunt
Amy Post
Catherine F. Stebbins
Mary Ann Frink
Lydia Mount
Delia Mathews
Catherine C. Paine
Elizabeth W. M'Clintock
Malvina Seymour
Phebe Mosher
Catherine Shaw
Deborah Scott
Sarah Hallowell
Mary M'Clintock
Mary Gilbert

Sophronia Taylor
Cynthia Davis
Hannah Plant
Lucy Jones
Sarah Whitney
Mary H. Hallowell
Elizabeth Conklin
Sally Pitcher
Mary Conklin
Susan Quinn
Mary S. Mirror
Phebe King
Julia Ann Drake
Charlotte Woodward
Martha Underhill
Dorothy Mathews
Eunice Barker
Sarah R. Woods
Lydia Gild
Sarah Hoffman
Elizabeth Leslie
Martha Ridley

Rachel D. Bonnel
Betsey Tewksbury
Rhoda Palmer
Margaret Jenkins
Cynthia Fuller
Mary Martin
P. A. Culvert
Susan R. Doty
Rebecca Race
Sarah A. Mosher
Mary E. Vail
Lucy Spalding
Lavina Latham
Sarah Smith
Eliza Martin
Maria E. Wilbur
Elizabeth D. Smith
Caroline Barker
Ann Porter
Experience Gibbs
Antoinette E. Segut
Hannah J. Latham
Sarah Sisson

GENTLEMEN:

Richard P. Hunt
Samuel D. Tillman
Justin Williams
Elisha Foote
Frederick Douglass
Henry W. Seymour
Henry Seymour
David Spalding
William G. Barker
Elias J. Doty
John Jones

William S. Dell
James Mott
William Burroughs
Robert Smallbridge
Jacob Mathews
Charles L. Hoskins
Thomas M'Clintock
Saron Phillips
Jacob P. Chamberlain
Jonathan Metcalf

Nathan J. Milliken
S. E. Woodworth
Edward F. Underhill
George W. Pryor
Joel Bunker
Isaac Van Tassel
Thomas Dell
E. W. Capron
Stephen Shear
Henry Hatley
Azaliah Schooley

The Seneca Falls Convention took place over 2 days—July 19 and July 20 in 1848. The Declaration of Sentiments was adopted by the convention on July 20.

SUSAN
B. Anthony

The Seneca Falls Convention led to more women's rights discussions and meetings. Shortly after, Elizabeth Cady Stanton met an important leader in the women's rights movement: Susan B. Anthony. Anthony's work in the temperance movement led her to forge a friendship with Stanton, who also held a leadership role in that movement. *"We were at once fast friends, in thought and sympathy we were one,"* Stanton remembered. They began to work together around 1851.

Stanton wrote speeches, letters, and newspaper articles but chose to stay at home to care for her growing family. (She would have seven children.) Anthony never married and traveled

Susan B. Anthony often stayed at the Stanton house to do work. Elizabeth's daughter Harriot remembered that Elizabeth was often *"entirely engrossed in writing a speech for Miss Anthony to deliver . . . while she kept the children out of sight and out of mind."* She and her siblings were afraid of Susan's strictness and punishments. But Anthony also cleaned scraped knees, pulled wagons, and stirred pots of soup. She became *"Aunt Susan"* after a time.

the country delivering Stanton's words to the public. Stanton later said, *"I forged the thunderbolts and she fired them."*

Stanton was the better writer, and Anthony was great at planning and organizing. Their different personalities and skills were an advantage in their friendship.

MORE TO KNOW

Susan B. Anthony said, *"I would not object to marriage if it were not that women throw away every plan and purpose of their own life, to conform to the plans and purposes of the man's life."*

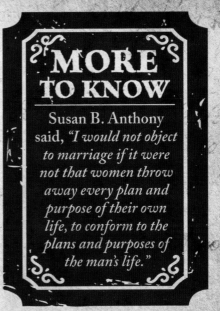

13

SPEECHES
and Issues

Elizabeth Cady Stanton's speeches touched on many topics, including temperance, justice, and equality. She thought men and women should be partners in marriage: *"There is one kind of marriage that has not been tried, and that is a contract made by equal parties to lead an equal life . . . Thus far, we have had man marriage and nothing more."* She also believed that women should be able to divorce husbands if they were treated badly.

Stanton advocated for more comfortable clothing for women, too. At that time, most women wore long, heavy, tight dresses and skirts. They could be uncomfortable and difficult to move in. Stanton sometimes wore bloomers, which were long pants, under a knee-length skirt. She said they made her feel *"like a captive set free."*

Also called reform skirts, bloomers were thought to be too immodest for "proper" women to wear. Though Amelia Bloomer didn't create this style of clothing, she was an advocate, and so the name stuck.

THE TEMPERANCE ISSUE

Women weren't welcome to speak or equally participate in men's temperance organizations. So, in 1852, Stanton and Anthony founded the Woman's State Temperance Society of New York. Their organization was criticized for focusing too much on women's right to vote on the temperance issue. Some also disagreed with a woman's right to divorce her husband if he abused alcohol. Though many people often thought Stanton went too far with many issues, she was unafraid of the public's view.

WORKING
for Abolition

MORE TO KNOW

In 1867, a New York Constitutional Convention committee stated about women's **suffrage**: *"Public sentiment does not demand and would not sustain an* **innovation** *so revolutionary and sweeping."*

In April 1861, the American Civil War began. The problems the war raised about states' rights and slavery turned attention away from the fight for women's equality. In 1862, the Stanton family moved to New York City, where Elizabeth Cady Stanton delivered speeches about abolition. In 1863, Stanton and Anthony formed the Women's Loyal National League, the first national women's political organization. About 5,000 women gathered 400,000 signatures to persuade Congress to pass the Thirteenth Amendment to abolish slavery, which it did in 1865.

However, Stanton became very upset when one of her friends and supporters, Wendell Phillips, argued in 1865 that a black man's right to vote was more important than a woman's right to vote. Stanton wrote to him: *"Do you believe the African race is composed entirely of males?"* She didn't think people had to choose one issue over the other.

A PETITION

FOR

UNIVERSAL SUFFRAGE.

To the Senate and House of Representatives:

The undersigned, Women of the United States, respectfully ask an amendment of the Constitution that shall prohibit the several States from disfranchising any of their citizens on the ground of sex.

In making our demand for Suffrage, we would call your attention to the fact that we represent fifteen million people—one half the entire population of the country—intelligent, virtuous, native-born American citizens; and yet stand outside the pale of political recognition.

The Constitution classes us as "free people," and counts us as whole persons in the basis of representation; and yet are we governed without our consent, compelled to pay taxes without appeal, and punished for violations of law without choice of judge or juror.

The experience of all ages, the Declarations of the Fathers, the Statute Laws of our own day, and the fearful revolution through which we have just passed, all prove the uncertain tenure of life, liberty and property so long as the ballot—the only weapon of self-protection—is not in the hand of every citizen.

Therefore, as you are now amending the Constitution, and, in harmony with advancing civilization, placing new safeguards round the individual rights of four millions of emancipated slaves, we ask that you extend the right of Suffrage to Woman—the only remaining class of disfranchised citizens—and thus fulfil your Constitutional obligation "to Guarantee, to every State in the Union a Republican form of Government."

As all partial application of Republican principles must ever breed a complicated legislation as well as a discontented people, we would pray your Honorable Body, in order to simplify the machinery of government and ensure domestic tranquillity, that you legislate hereafter for persons, citizens, tax-payers, and not for class or caste.

For justice and equality your petitioners will ever pray.

NAMES.	RESIDENCE.
Elizabeth Stanton,	New York
Susan B. Anthony	Rochester – N.Y.
Antoinette Brown Blackwell	New York
Lucy Stone	Newark N. Jersey
Joanna S. Moore	48 Livingston. Brooklyn
Ernestine L. Rose	New York
Harriet E. Eaton	6 West 4th Street N.Y.
Catharine C. Wilkeson	83 Clinton Place New York
Elizabeth C. Tilton	48 Livingston St. Brooklyn
Mary Fowler Gilbert	205 W. 19 St New York
Mary C. Gilbert	New York
M. Griffith	New York.

THE AERA

In 1866, Stanton and other suffragists formed a new organization: the American Equal Rights Association (AERA). The AERA included many abolitionists, and its members hoped at first to help both blacks and women win the right to vote. However, the organization became divided. Some people thought that fighting for suffrage for both would cause failure for both. They thought blacks must be given the right to vote first. The group fell apart by 1869.

This 1866 petition from Stanton, Anthony, and others urged Congress to allow women and black men to vote.

UNSTEADY
Allies

DIVISION

Many in the AERA, including President Lucretia Mott, were angry about Stanton and Anthony accepting money from a racist. Stanton and Anthony urged the organization to support an amendment for women's rights, as well as the Fifteenth Amendment, which would give black men the right to vote. Many members refused. So, in 1869, Stanton and Anthony established the National Woman Suffrage Association to fight for an amendment for women's suffrage, making it a priority over suffrage for African American men.

Elizabeth Cady Stanton and Susan B. Anthony needed money to continue their efforts. So, they accepted the help of George Francis Train. The good news was that Train was extremely rich and eager to help the women and their cause. The bad news was that Train was a **racist**. Stanton was aware that *"we have shocked our old friends . . . Time will show that Miss Anthony and I are neither idiots nor lunatics."*

George Francis Train

MORE TO KNOW

Stanton later admitted: *"Susan & I were so desperate we said to each other when considering Train's proposition 'Yes we would work with the Devil if he would advocate our cause.'"*

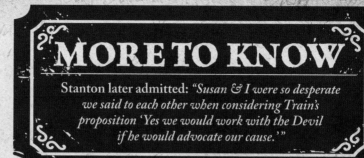

The Revolution.

PRINCIPLE, NOT POLICY: JUSTICE, NOT FAVORS.—MEN, THEIR RIGHTS AND NOTHING MORE: WOMEN, THEIR RIGHTS AND NOTHING LESS.

NEW YORK, WEDNESDAY, JANUARY 15, 1868.

VOL. I.—NO. 2. $2.00 A YEAR.

TEXAS RECONSTRUCTION.

SCARCELY a week passes in which there are not frequent murders in Texas of Union men, officers as well as others, white as well as black, and generally they go unavenged, the murderers even boasting of their bloody work! The San Antonio *Express* states that on Friday, Nov. 15, Capt. C. E. Culver, the Bureau Agent stationed at Cotton Gin, Freestone County, and his orderly, were murdered three miles north of Springfield, Limestone County. It appears that Capt. Culver had some little difficulty with one Wm. Stewart, and this same Stewart claims to have killed both Capt. Culver and his orderly, and says they fired on him first; but, strange to say, they were shot with different guns. Capt. Culver's head was also cut asunder—done with an axe or some other sharp instrument. There was a large bullet-hole through his right breast, and there was no hole in the shirts or vest Capt. Culver had on at the time he was killed. It is strange that a large ball should pass through a man's body and not through the clothes he had on at the time. It is a great mystery. Capt. Culver was an active member of the Union League of America, and was to open a Council

path—amending the Constitution—but thus far without success. The vote in 1846 was 85,406 for, and 224,336 against impartial suffrage; in 1860 there were 197,503 in favor, and 337,984 opposed.

"The question is naturally up again in the present Convention, and may in due time come before the people; but past experience gives little hope for the friends of impartial suffrage. In the votes noted above, the Democratic party conspicuously opposed the repeal of the property qualification; a few, doubtless, voted the right way, but where one Democrat voted 'Yes,' probably ten Republicans voted 'No.'"

HOME TRUTHS.

ELIZA ARCHARD, in the *Herald of Health* has a long article, full of wholesome Rye and Indian truths, like these below—good for kitchen or parlor.

If one should say: "Muscle and Manhood," it would be nothing either strange or unusual, merely an alliteration for the well recognized fact that man is an animal. For muscle and manhood run together by nature. But who ever heard of muscular womanhood? Nobody

gentleman was a man of average muscle; the four girls, as ladies go, had decidedly more than the average of physical strength.

And this is what four full-grown girls amount to! But something very like the millennium will approach before women can be made to understand that they ought to be ashamed to let one man have more strength than four women. This is the work of it all. It is their *religious conviction* that the crowning glory of womankind is physical degeneracy. Their chief delight is to believe themselves born to cling to whatever is nearest, and to be droopy, like the ivy-to-the-oak way, and to be viney, and twiney, and whiney throughout. Like the ivy to the oak, exactly, if we are willing to learn anything from nature; for, in point of fact, the ivy generally smothers the oak to death at last.

"Woman conquers by her weakness." Woman's weakness, indeed! Woman's nonsense! Woman's weakness is despicable. Weakness of any kind is a credit to nobody. How can it be? Do we admire a man more because one arm is paralyzed, or because he is blind of an eye? Is there anything particularly lovely in the ghastly sight of a man who is starving to death? And what more claim to our admiration has a

One reporter said that, while Elizabeth Cady Stanton looked like a kindly grandmother, her words were like "gun shots." She was the primary writer of The Revolution.

Train promised them money to begin a women's rights newspaper. Called *The Revolution*, it first appeared in January 1868. However, Train was later jailed in Ireland, and the funding ended. The women had to give up the paper by 1870.

"ONE AND *Inseparable*"

MORE TO KNOW

Stanton's friend Theodore Tilton said in 1871: *"It has been sometimes suspected that Mrs. Stanton and Miss Anthony are two distinct persons . . . I remain of the opinion that, like Liberty and Union, they are 'one and inseparable.'"*

The friendship between Elizabeth Cady Stanton and Susan B. Anthony wasn't always smooth. When *The Revolution* stopped publication, it owed about $10,000 in debts. Stanton refused to pay. So, Anthony was forced to pay it off by herself slowly over the course of several years.

In the 1870s, Stanton had fewer family duties and so began to travel and give speeches. Newspapers criticized Anthony's speaking while praising Stanton's. Stanton was at ease with a crowd and often funny, while Anthony was serious and sometimes awkward. The *San Francisco Chronicle* described: *"Whilst the one is gifted with wonderful **oratorical** powers. . . the other is hesitating and halty."* Stanton didn't always defend her friend.

While these things strained their friendship, they were quick to make up after arguments and get back to work *"as if nothing ever happened,"* according to Stanton's daughter Margaret.

Henry Stanton once remarked to his wife, "You stir up Susan and she stirs the world."

FRIENDS FOR LIFE

In 1890, Elizabeth Cady Stanton said of her relationship with Susan B. Anthony: *"If there is one part of my life that gives me more intense satisfaction than any other, it is my friendship of forty years' standing with Susan B. Anthony."* Anthony later recalled: *"I want you to understand that I could never have done the work I have if I had not had that woman [Stanton] at my right hand."*

21

EXTREME
Measures

The Fourteenth Amendment was passed in 1868. It stated that "all persons" born in the United States were citizens and were guaranteed the rights that citizens had, including the right to vote. Stanton and Anthony took the position that the amendment gave women the right to vote, since they're "persons." The government disagreed. When Susan B. Anthony voted in 1872, she was arrested and jailed. Stanton tried to vote in 1880, but the official took away her ballot before she could cast it.

In the 1870s, Stanton found a reformer more extreme than herself. Victoria Woodhull supported many shocking issues, including a world government and ending marriage. She also supported women's suffrage. Stanton's

MAKING THE PATH SMOOTHER

It wasn't easy for Elizabeth Cady Stanton to leave her children, and her children hated to be away from their mother. But Stanton had them in mind. She once wrote: *"I feel that I am doing an immense amount of good in rousing women to thought and inspiring them with new hope and self-respect, that I am making the path smoother for you."* Stanton wanted to continue *"teaching woman her duties to herself."*

enthusiasm for Woodhull cooled once she realized she wasn't as interested in promoting women's rights as in her own presidential campaign.

Victoria Woodhull (standing) reads an argument in favor of women's suffrage to the Judiciary Committee of the House of Representatives in 1871.

MORE TO KNOW

In 1872, Victoria Woodhull used the National Woman Suffrage Association meeting as an opportunity to launch her run as a US presidential candidate.

100 YEARS
Without the Vote

In 1876, 100 years after the United States declared freedom from England, Stanton, Anthony, and Matilda Gage wrote a Declaration of Rights of the Women of the United States. They asked to be an official part of the July 4 celebration in Philadelphia, Pennsylvania. They were denied as those in charge thought the speech would overshadow the joyous occasion.

MORE TO KNOW

While Anthony read the declaration, Stanton and Lucretia Mott held the National Woman Suffrage Association's annual meeting in a nearby church.

While Stanton refused to go to the ceremony, Anthony and others passed out copies of the statement. Next, without permission, Anthony read the declaration aloud from a platform: *"While the nation is **buoyant** with patriotism, and all hearts are attuned to praise, it is with sorrow we come to strike the one **discordant** note, on this 100th anniversary of our country's birth."* She then reminded the crowd of women's lack of rights.

The suffragists acted as the Founding Fathers had in continuing to demand what was rightfully theirs.

"WE ASK..."

The end of the Declaration of Rights of the Women of the United States stated: *"We ask justice, we ask equality, we ask that all the civil and political rights that belong to citizens of the United States, be guaranteed to us and our daughters forever."* Even while General Joseph Hawley denied them the right to officially speak, he admitted: *"Undoubtedly we have not lived up to our own original Declaration of Independence in many respects."*

The FINAL YEARS

In 1890, the National Woman Suffrage Association and the American Woman Suffrage Association joined to become the National American Woman Suffrage Association (NAWSA). Stanton became its president, though she was increasingly losing supporters because of her demand for equality in many issues. In her first speech, she said: *"We do not want to limit our platform to bare suffrage and nothing more. We must demand equality everywhere in Church and State."* She also wanted to advocate for all races.

Stanton grew discouraged with the NAWSA's narrow goals. Her health was failing, too: *"I cannot trot 100 feet without puffing."* She stepped down as

THE WOMAN'S BIBLE

Stanton's challenge to Christianity was called *The Woman's Bible*. She, along with numerous other authors, wrote it in two parts. Many in the NAWSA feared it would harm the cause of women's suffrage. They thought it was going too far to dispute the stories, beliefs, and traditions of various religions. Stanton believed that, as the Bible was sometimes used to keep women from gaining equality, some parts should be challenged or even rewritten.

president in 1892. She turned to a project that had long interested her: writing a book challenging some passages in the Bible concerning women.

Elizabeth's actual signature:

The Woman's Bible became a bestseller. This is an early draft.

LASTING
Legacy

Elizabeth Cady Stanton kept busy in her old age. *"I am always busy,"* she said. *"Perhaps that is why I am always well."* She died at the age of 87 on October 26, 1902. She had planned her own funeral. The service was conducted by a woman. At the head of her coffin was the table on which she had written the Declaration of Sentiments. And on the coffin was a picture of her lifelong friend Susan B. Anthony. Anthony died almost 4 years after Stanton on March 13, 1906.

Sadly, neither woman lived long enough to see women gain the right to vote. Undeniably, they had done much of the hard work to get the nation to finally accept the idea. The Nineteenth Amendment, guaranteeing women's suffrage, was finally passed on August 18, 1920.

TIMELINE
THE LIFE OF
ELIZABETH CADY STANTON

Born November 12 in Johnstown, New York — **1815**

1830 — Begins to attend Troy Female Seminary

Marries Henry Stanton and attends World's Antislavery Convention — **1840**

1848 — Seneca Falls Convention takes place

Begins to work with Susan B. Anthony — **1851**

1852 — Helps found Woman's State Temperance Society of New York

Helps establish Women's Loyal National League — **1863**

1866 — Helps form the American Equal Rights Association

Begins to write for *The Revolution* — **1868**

1869 — Helps to establish National Woman Suffrage Association

Helps write Declaration of Rights of the Women of the United States — **1876**

1880 — Tries to vote

Becomes president of National American Woman Suffrage Association — **1890**

1902 — Dies October 26

Nineteenth Amendment becomes law — **1920**

CREATORS AND WRITERS OF HISTORY

Besides being a force of change for women's rights, Stanton was also a recorder of its history. She, Anthony, and Matilda Gage were the first authors to work on the multivolume *History of Woman Suffrage*. They worked for 4 years to finish three books, which included letters, newsletters, and speeches. Stanton finished the third book in 1885 and then stopped to take care of her husband Henry, who died in 1887. Three more volumes were written later.

GLOSSARY

abridge: to take away

advocate: to support or speak in favor of something

buoyant: cheerful and hopeful

convention: a gathering of people who have a common interest or profession

discordant: in disagreement

engross: to take up someone's whole attention

innovation: a new way of doing things

oblivious: unaware of or paying no attention to somebody or something

obstinately: stubbornly or unwillingly

oratorical: relating to the art of speaking in public

racist: one who looks down on people of other races

seminary: a school for girls

suffrage: the right to vote

temperance: avoiding the drinking of alcohol